TEEN-AGERS
PR

TEEN-AGERS
PRAY

CONCORDIA PUBLISHING HOUSE
SAINT LOUIS, MISSOURI

Copyright © 1955 by Concordia Publishing House

St. Louis, Missouri

Twenty-first Printing 1974

Library of Congress Catalog Card No. 55-12193

ISBN 0-570-03018-8

MANUFACTURED IN THE UNITED STATES OF AMERICA

24 25 26 27 28 29 30 31 32 33   PP   89 88 87 86 85 84 83 82 81 80

PREFACE

God's call to prayer is so inviting that a Christian cannot but pray. God's promises are so sure that we should never doubt His answer to prayer. *Teen-Agers Pray* is intended to help young people express their faith in prayer.

We can do God no greater honor than to ask for hard things and to trust that He will hear us. Doubt about God's ability or willingness to help us shows a lack of faith. It is really a dishonor to our almighty and loving God. Faith is trust and confidence. By trusting in God we honor Him.

God's promise to hear our prayers does not mean, of course, that God will give us anything we ask. At times He may have to deny our requests for our good. God loves us. He knows what is good for us. We do not always know what is good for us, and so we ask for things which we do not need or which would be harmful to us. For example: If we asked God for riches, He might know that riches would weaken or destroy our faith. Should God still give us riches? Out of love for us He will deny our request for riches. There are other things which are good in themselves, but which might not be good for us. In refusing to give them to us, God really hears our prayer to do what is best for us.

When we are praying for stronger faith and a Christian life, we know that we are praying that God's will may be done. We know God will hear our prayer. When we pray for an earthly blessing, we say: "Give it to me, Lord, if it is good for me. If You have to deny my request, I will love You just the same." By such prayer we lay the matter entirely into God's hands. We surrender completely to Him, knowing that all is well when He rules our lives. We pray properly when we ask what God wants, not what we want. God always hears such prayer, and it brings us greater blessings than all the riches of the world could bring.

It is not always easy to surrender so completely to God, but it becomes easier as we practice it. It brings us peace and joy to pray that way. As long as we keep trusting in God, praying and surrendering ourselves to Him, we will have a successful life on earth, and eternal life, too. We are able to do this as long as we know and believe God's Word.

The prayers in this book take surrender to God for granted. A Christian would not want it any other way. It is hoped that the book will stimulate the prayer life of the young people who use it.

The prayers cover the problems and concerns of teenagers. They were written by people who understand the needs of young people, and some were written by teenagers. All prayers were read by teen-agers, and many of the prayers were read aloud to them. Many helpful suggestions were received in this way. Also the title of the book was selected by a group of young people with whom the prayers were discussed.

Twenty-eight people participated in the writing of the book, most of them pastors and teachers who work constantly with young people. The contributors are Julius W. Acker, Elmer A. Arnst, Victor A. Bartelt, Martin H. Einspahr, Theo. Gerken, Eugene F. Gruell, Elmer H. Huedepohl, Frederick W. Ibeling, Edwin A. Jiede, P. Arthur Juergensen, Edward J. Keuer, Howard W. Kramer, Wm. A.

Kramer, Elaine Kruse, Margaret Kruse, Martin F. Luebke, Walter A. Maier, Jr., Guido A. Merkens, Frederick A. Meyer, Herbert C. Moldenhauer, Frederick H. Pralle, Walter Riess, James O. Roberts, Roland H. Seboldt, Paul Ph. Spitz, Wm. Urbrook, Elmer N. Witt, and Martin J. Zschoche. Allan H. Jahsmann and Walter Riess read the manuscript critically. The book was outlined and edited by Wm. A. Kramer.

A book of prayers can at best be only a guide for the user. There will be many occasions where the young Christian will have to speak to God out of his own heart. In connection with almost any prepared prayer a Christian will want to tell God his own joys and needs. It is the hope and prayer of all who had a part in preparing *Teen-Agers Pray* that the book will help stimulate Christian youth in their conversation with God.

THE PUBLISHER

CONTENTS

PREFACE

PRAYERS FOR MANY NEEDS

For Trust in God 2
For Forgiveness of Sins 3
For a Thankful Heart 4
For the Holy Spirit 5
For the Holy Spirit 6
For Dedication to God 7
For Strength in Temptation 8
For Faithfulness 9
For Patience in Trouble 10
For a Cheerful Outlook on Life 11
For Self-Control 12
For Courage 13
For Help to Love Others 14
Before a Date 15
After a Date 16
For Help in Finding Good Friends 17
For Health and Usefulness 18
For Guidance in Choosing a Vocation 19
For Success in School 20
For Power to Go On 21
For Joy in Witnessing 22
When Feeling Low 23
In Sickness 24

ix

PRAYERS FOR SPECIAL DAYS

Thanksgiving Day	26
Christmas	27
New Year's Day	28
Lent	29
Easter	30
Ascension Day	31
Pentecost	32
Independence Day	33
Birthday	34

PRAYERS ON THE COMMANDMENTS

For the Right Love for God	36
For Reverence	37
For Joy in Worship	38
For Obedience to Parents	39
For Love for the Neighbor	40
For Purity of Heart and Life	41
For Honesty	42
For a Kind Tongue	43
For Contentment	44

PRAYERS ON THE PETITIONS OF THE LORD'S PRAYER

That God's Name May Be Hallowed	46
For the Coming of God's Kingdom	47
That God's Will May Be Done	48
For Daily Bread	49
For Forgiveness of Sins	50
For Help in Temptation	51
For Deliverance from Evil	52

PRAYERS FOR THE WEEK

    Sunday   54

    Monday   55

    Tuesday   56

    Wednesday   57

    Thursday   58

    Friday   59

    Saturday   60

    Luther's Morning Prayer   61

    Luther's Evening Prayer   62

TABLE PRAYERS

    Before Meals   64

    After Meals   65

MISCELLANEOUS PRAYERS

    For Giving Myself Completely to God   68

    For Joy in Being a Christian   69

    For the Conversion of the Unbelievers   70

    For the Church   71

    For a Creative Life   72

    Thanks for the Gift of Heaven   73

    Thanks for Being a Christian   74

    For Blessings Through Baptism   75

    Before the Sacrament   76

    Before the Sacrament   77

    A Thank-You for the Beautiful World   78

    Before a Trip   79

    For My Friends   80

    Make Me an Instrument of Peace   81

    Lord, Teach Me How   82

PRAYERS *for Many Needs*

For Trust in God

Dear heavenly Father, I want to be brave and trusting, and I want to do great things for You. You have promised to help me do great things by faith, even to move mountains if necessary. Thank You for the faith which You have given me and for all that You have done with me and through me. But often my faith is so weak that I get worried about it. When I find life difficult, doubts and fears arise in my heart. But I know You can keep me in faith. You can make me strong. You can and will help me to accomplish my tasks at home, in school, at my job, and in church, and You will finally take me to heaven.

In reading my Bible I find that young people like Joseph and David seemed to have no fear at all. They simply trusted in Your strength to see them through their difficulties. Dear God, I want to be like them. I pray, therefore, that You will help me to have a strong faith. Make me sure of my salvation. Help me to believe that You can do all things.

Teach me to know that Your way is always right, and give me the confidence and strength to walk Your way. Never let my will clash with Yours, but help me to meet every challenge head-on, so that, like heroes of faith before me, I, too, may be among those who gained a victory for You. This I ask for Jesus' sake. Amen.

For Forgiveness of Sins

Heavenly Father, I confess my many sins and shortcomings. With the publican I say, "God, be merciful to me, a sinner." Despite my efforts to do no wrong, my self-examination shows that I have had evil thoughts, that I have spoken evil words and done much else that was wrong. Forgive all of this through Jesus' blood and merit. I trust in You, because You have said there is forgiveness with You.

Dear Lord, I need Your help every minute of the day. I want above all to do what is right. Begin with my heart, Lord, and fill it with Your thinking. Make my heart over, and help me to prefer what You prefer. Make Your desires my desires. Let there be room only for the right thoughts. Be with my mouth, that when I speak, I say only things that You want me to say. Grant that I may give help and encouragement to those around me. Let my hands be Your hands, that what I do will serve others and will be a credit to You. I ask all this in the name of Jesus. Amen.

For a Thankful Heart

Dear Father in heaven, every time I open my eyes I see things that You have given me — home and clothes, friends and school, a free country, luxuries from science and industry; and every time I hear Your Word I see more gifts from Your loving hand — a well-planned world, promises for guidance, protection from evil, forgiveness for every sin of mine and for the sins of others, and the promise of heaven; I see new life and joy in Christ, my Savior.

Yet I know that I do not think about these things enough, dear Lord. I am so busy with school and sports and work and having fun that I forget them easily. Give me a thankful heart that I may be more conscious of Your daily love for me. And give me a useful life that I may honestly show my thankfulness in all that I am and do.

Hear me, dear God, for the sake of Jesus. Amen.

For the Holy Spirit

Life gets so complicated, O Jesus. Every day there is so much to be decided and said and done, and often I get confused.

Life gets so discouraging, dear Lord. I see so much that is bad in the world, in the people I know, and in myself.

Life gets so routine, O Christ. I take things for granted and coast along from day to day doing so little for Your kingdom.

Send Your Spirit, O Jesus, to guide me in this mixed-up world through the understanding of the Scriptures. Send Your Spirit, dear Lord, to tell me there is forgiveness through Your life and death and resurrection. Send Your Spirit, O Christ, to excite me about the things that really count, especially about my own eternal salvation and that of others.

At home and at school, on the street and at work, on a date and by myself, I need the power of Your Spirit, that my whole life on earth may be good and useful, and that my hope of heaven may remain strong and sure. Hear me, O Savior. Amen.

For the Holy Spirit

My life is dark and uninspired without Your Spirit, eternal Christ. Moments of boredom go by so terribly slow when You seem far from me. Please send me Your Holy Spirit, that I may turn these dead hours into exciting adventures with You and for You.

I miss my opportunities to talk about You. I slip down into the humdrum of the things around me. I do not pray or think of You. Come, Holy Ghost, God and Lord! Forgive me my spiritual laziness, and in spite of it give me the great gift of Your life and fire.

O Lord, I wait for You. I pray for You. Take me and use me however You wish. Yours I am, now and always. Inspire me with Your own light, Jesus Christ, Giver of all life!

I believe that I shall live Your life — under Your Spirit. Amen.

For Dedication to God

Dearest Lord Jesus, because You have bought me with Your precious blood, I am Your own, and my life, filled with youthful energy, belongs to You. Let me, therefore, never yield to the thought that I can live my life as I please, nor let me waste my time and energy in earthly pleasures and amusements, or with activities that now seem so important but are of no value to my future life.

Help me, rather, to dedicate my life to You, and to remember that, since I am Your child, I have a duty and responsibility to serve You and my fellow men. Give me courage to witness for You, to speak to others about You, and to conduct myself at all times according to Your holy Law, which I have willingly chosen as the guide for my entire life.

Help me at all times to want what You want and to do what You want me to do. Increase my desire to serve You by the Holy Spirit, and by Your holy Word show me how I can best follow Your guidance and direction. Amen.

For Strength in Temptation

Lord, the world is all around me — on top and beneath and even inside of me. I cannot move without seeing what I should not have seen, hearing what I should never have heard, doing what had better never been done. Before I know it, I am tied up hand and foot with my own desires.

For this forgive me, Savior. Forgive me my wandering eyes. Forgive me for forgetting whose I am when I walk into the world and join the world — instead of going through it with You at my side.

My only hope in all this, Lord, is Your strength. I cannot hope to win my fights against my temptations without the ammunition of Your presence, Your Word and Sacraments, Your comfort in defeat. Build me up, my Savior, to meet head-on the temptations which I will face. Make me a winner in the fight, for Your sake!

I love You more than anyone or anything else, Lord Jesus, in the world or out of it. Amen.

For Faithfulness

Dear Lord, with a thankful heart I praise You, my Maker, my Savior, the Giver and Protector of my Christian faith and life. By myself I am weak and helpless. My own power is nothing. With Jacob I must say, "I am not worthy of the least of all the mercies and of all the truth which You have showed to Your servant." But with You I have strength and salvation. Help me always to live as a believer should, trusting in Your promises and blessings for all my needs.

Temptations bother me every day. Often my faith gets weak, and I give in to sin. Give me the strength to confess my sins and the confidence that You will forgive them. Forgive me for the sake of Jesus Christ, my Savior. Be with me, guide me, help me in all I think, say, and do. Let no danger of body or soul tear me away from You. Keep me firm in faith and loyal in loving service until the angels take me to heaven. Use me to lead others to You and to salvation. Bless my prayer, through Jesus Christ. Amen.

For Patience in Trouble

O Lord Jesus, I am often perplexed by troubles. I have so many doubts about myself. I do not always get along with other people as I should. I wish I had more friends. I wish I could always obey my parents and teachers and get along with my brothers and sisters and with my schoolmates.

Because You are my Savior, I pray, kindly help me according to Your will. Forgive my doubts and sins, and give me courage. Make me humble. Help me to appreciate other people as I should, that I may understand them and like them. Show me how to be friendly and patient, even when people make me angry. Most of all, grant that I apply myself to my studies in school, that now and when I am older I may be someone worthwhile. Make me useful to You and to those around me.

Keep me, O Jesus, calm and cheerful when I am in trouble, for I know that You are with me. Thank You, Jesus. Amen.

For a Cheerful Outlook on Life

Gracious and loving Savior, You have encouraged me with the words: "Be of good cheer; I have overcome the world." Grant me the Holy Spirit that I may cheerfully and confidently place my hand in Yours and follow Your safe guidance through life's problems and pleasures. Help me more clearly to see You and Your love amid my joys and sorrows, pleasures and pains, triumphs and trials. Help me to regard all these but as hills and valleys on the path which You have chosen for me, a path which rises ever upward to the glorious mansions which You have prepared for me above.

Lead me to the assurance that as You have overcome the world, so You will also help me to overcome whatever troubles beset me along life's way. With this confidence I, too, can be of good cheer, serving You with Christlike joy and spreading cheer to others, ever mindful that my path leads but to heaven and You. I will then also be able to praise You in my trouble, knowing that "all things work together for good to them that love God." This grant me for Your own sake. Amen.

For Self-Control

Dear Savior, I admire the calmness and self-control which You showed under trying circumstances, even in Your suffering. I want to be more like You. Grant that I may more fully dedicate my body, mind, and will to Your service. Help me to follow You more perfectly in thought, word, and deed. Show me how to work for You, for my fellow believers, and for all who need my help. Make me both willing and glad to do so.

Give me the virtues of sympathy, patience, fairness, and purity. Keep far from me the weaknesses of selfishness, envy, stubbornness, and pride. Keep me from a quick temper and from a discourteous disregard for the feelings of my fellow men.

So bend my will that I may avoid all forms of evil and do only such deeds as true children of God may do.

O Lord, so control my entire body, mind, and will that I may be a living witness of the faith that lives in me and that I may glorify Your saving name. Amen.

For Courage

O Lord, my God, great and good, I come to You in my weakness, and I know You will understand. I want to tell You how weak and afraid I am. You have tried to make me strong by giving me great tasks and by Your promise that You will never leave me nor forsake me, but I have failed the challenge many a day. Sometimes I get so discouraged with my weakness that I am afraid I cannot go on being a Christian.

O God, my Father, comfort me with the assurance that You still love me and that You will forgive me in Jesus, Your Son. Make me more like Him. Reach down and take hold of my hand, and lift me to great heights of strength. Inspire me with noble thoughts and ambitions.

Give me the courage to speak when I should, to keep silent when silence is better, to face life as it is, and to dedicate each new day to You.

Give me the wisdom to see the possibilities of holy service, and then grant me a strong will to dare to do everything that needs to be done. Your will, not mine, be done, O Lord. Use me to accomplish Your purpose in Christ. Amen.

For Help to Love Others

My Father in heaven, it is good to come to You. You are a welcome Refuge from the hate and jealousies of the world. In Your fellowship I find peace and quiet and a love that is pure. When I am near You, I can be calm and composed, even though people around me may be bitter and loveless. Forgive me that I so often forget Your nearness and become the victim of anger or ill will. Help me to rejoice in the good fortune of others, instead of being selfish and jealous. I need Your help. Make me humble, grateful, and peaceable.

O Lord, You are so holy in Your love and so forgiving in Your mercy! Make me more like You. Give me the power to love people with a charity that overlooks their faults and pardons every ill will. Give me the grace to smile when I want to cry, and to forgive when I want to fight back. As you have shown me Your love in Jesus, so help me to live in love with all men. In the name of Jesus. Amen.

Before a Date

For my partner today, Lord Christ, I want to thank You. How much You must love me to give me friends, wonderful times, talks and laughs, and everything else You have given me through my dates!

Lord, I want You to know that I love You also. And I want to tell You that out of my love for You I will treat my date right. I will try to help my date by being a companion who builds happiness. I will try to be genial and mannerly, and so lead my friend to enjoy our time together. I will do nothing to hurt or tear down my friend's character morally or spiritually — through my own desires or by giving in to my friend's. In all this, my Lord and Savior, I know I may weaken and fail. But I also know that You will be with me, Lord, in the car, wherever I go. That is why, before this date, I want to ask You for the kind of power only You can put into me — power to live up to my love for You, power to love others, help others, and build up others, because I love You above all and first of all. Please send Me Your power to be a real friend on this date, my Lord. Amen.

After a Date

Thanks, Lord, for giving me a partner today. Thanks for a good time. Thanks for going along with me.

If I have said anything or done anything to offend You or my date, forgive me. My Savior, strengthen me to do and say right things, to be more completely Your own. Make me more courteous when I am with others, and keep me sure of myself — because I know You.

I ask that I might have many happy times on dates, Lord. Send me opportunities to be with others. Let me be loved, and let me love my friends — and You forever.

There is nothing more I want than to be Yours all the time. Amen.

For Help in Finding Good Friends

Lord Jesus, You have lived on earth and have not forgotten the value of companionship and the good that comes from having true friends. You provided a Jonathan for David and a Ruth for Naomi. So lead me to find friends who will love me in spite of what I am, friends who will help bring out the best that is in me. Give me the kind of friends who will bring lasting happiness into my life.

Since I do not want to flirt with temptation, give me a faith that will turn away from shady friendships, a faith that will seek close companions among those who share my beliefs and who live their life for You.

Give me eyes to see the needs of my friends and a heart that is loyal to them. Give me understanding, that I may learn to laugh with the happy and to sympathize with those who are in trouble.

And if all earthly friendships should fail, assure me always that You are still my Friend, a Friend who loves me when I am not lovable, who understands me when no one else understands.

I ask this of You, because You loved me first and because You are the truest Friend of all. Amen.

For Health and Usefulness

O almighty God, You have made man, and You preserve him, and I know that I depend on You for everything. Help me always to remember that You are my Creator and the Creator of all things, and that my body is the temple of the Holy Spirit. Grant the gift of health to me in these important years, that with a sound mind and body I may serve You. Help me to use the special blessings of my age — its youth and vigor — as fit tools in the building of Your kingdom. Remove all illnesses or accidents which would deprive me of these means or which would lessen their usefulness. And keep me thankful for the health which You have given.

At the same time, dear Lord, keep me aware of the responsibilities which I owe to the mind and body which You have given me. Give me a sensible attitude toward the necessary rules of health, especially in these years when so many forms of study and activity are a part of my life. Teach me to know that an overtaxed or neglected body or mind can never serve You efficiently or well.

This I ask, in the name of Your dear Son, who went about doing good. Amen.

For Guidance in Choosing a Vocation

Almighty and everlasting God, You have commanded all to work and to be useful. Help me to see that work is a privilege and a blessing. Help me in Your infinite love and with Your divine guidance to choose the right vocation, one that is right for me. You know what is good for me, because You are so much wiser than I am. Guide me in choosing a vocation in which I may use my best abilities of mind and body, one in which I will find an interest and satisfaction in my duties, and one in which I will best perform a service to my fellow men.

Help me, O Lord, as I make my choice, to remember that the most important consideration is my service to You and Your kingdom. Teach me to know that no matter how humble my tasks or exalted my position in life, it is always to be an expression of my faith and of love for You. Grant this, I pray, for the sake of Your Son, my dear Savior. Amen.

For Success in School

Dear Lord Jesus, perfect Teacher, Wisest of the wise, You lived on our earth, and You remember Your own days of growing and learning. Help me in my preparations, not only to gain new information, but to grow in real wisdom.

I do not ask You to give me the highest grades or the highest test scores in the class, but rather a clear mind that will make my own best possible.

Save me from selfish pride that would lord my successes over my classmates; rather, give me the desire to help those who find it hard to learn.

Also You know the power of temptation. Deliver me from the drag of laziness that poisons the spirit. Keep me from trying to make my way by cheating. Help me to remember that there is no easy way to success. Open my eyes and understanding to see the wonders of Your world and the goodness of Your grace.

As I grow in learning, make of me a sharp and powerful tool, fully equipped to perform Your holy will in this world. Help me also in my growing years to see clearly the earthly calling that You would have me follow.

I ask all this of You, not because I have succeeded before, but because I know I need You now. Amen.

For Power to Go On

Why am I so weak, Lord and Savior? When I think I am going strong, then I start to fail. When I want so much to keep going for You, I sputter out and weaken. My body and my mind climb hills — only to come down again into deep valleys.

Lord, have mercy on me. As You fed Elijah in the wilderness, so fill me with Your energy. Let my strength mount up as an eagle soaring into the sky. Let me feel Your power guiding me when my poor strength is gone.

That power, Lord, which You radiated from Your cross — that power I ask of You right now. Bring it into my life and let it rule me. Raise my sagging spirits with fresh food and drink from heaven itself. Sharpen my faith to grab hold of You when weakness comes.

Savior, be my Fortress, be my Power. I love You, and I believe. Amen.

For Joy in Witnessing

Dear heavenly Father, I cannot understand that You have asked me, a sinner, to help in teaching Your Word. How wonderful that I can tell the glad news of salvation to my friends and others! Help me to live in such a way that people will know that I am a Christian. Help me to speak so they will know that I mean it. In words and deeds help me to show that I love You.

As opportunities present themselves, help me for Jesus' sake to speak up with courage. Help me to do it joyfully and convincingly for my Savior. Let me never be ashamed of Christ and His Gospel, even if people should ridicule me or if they should resent my invitation to faith and salvation. Use me in Your own way to bring the knowledge of Christ to many who do not yet know the peace and power which He brings to the human heart. In His name I pray. Amen.

When Feeling Low

How heavy my heart can get, Lord! It seems that I have lost everything — every hope and every happiness — and all that's left is tired, worn-out days and hours.

Lord, sometimes I think I've even lost You, so low I feel — as if You had left me alone and didn't care.

O Savior, tell me that isn't so.

And come near, come real close, my Lord. Whisper again into my heart those warm words of forgiveness, love, and promise. Fill me with yearning for You — and then fill my yearning with You.

Savior, my Savior, I trust You to lift me. I believe. Help me out of my unbelief. Even so come, Lord Jesus! Amen.

In Sickness

Dear Lord, my heavenly Physician, help me to realize that this sickness is meant for my good, since You have promised that "all things work together for good to them that love God."

Help me to continue to trust in You, as Job did, regardless of how terrible the pain or how uncomfortable I may be.

Restore me to good health as soon as it is good for me. To that end, bless the efforts of all those who are trying to help me recover.

If it is Your will that I should recover, help me show my gratitude by leading a more godly life. However, if it is Your will that I should die, take me to heaven, where there is no sickness, pain, or sin. I pray in the name of Jesus. Amen.

PRAYERS *for Special Days*

Thanksgiving Day

I thank You, Lord, for everything. You have given me my life, my body and soul, my skills and abilities, and all that I am. You have given me my family and my friends. Because of Your goodness and kindness You have blessed me with plenty to eat and to wear, a home in which to live, and a world to enjoy. You have put me in this wonderful land of liberty, where I can go to Your house and worship You any time without fear of imprisonment or death. For all these physical blessings, thanks, Lord.

I do not deserve Your blessings at all, Lord, because I am a terrible sinner. Please forgive my sins, especially the sin of thanklessness, through Christ Jesus, my Savior, whom You have put in my heart by faith. I thank You for my Savior, for my faith, for the forgiveness of sins, for my eternal life and salvation, for my church, and all my spiritual blessings. As I give my thanks to You, Lord, grant me a greater love for You, so that I may live my thanks by serving You with more of my time, talents, and treasure in my home, my church, my school, and my community. In Jesus' name. Amen.

Christmas

Dear Child in the Manger, I am happy that on the first Christmas Eve You came down from heaven to be born of Mary, the virgin meek and mild, and to be my precious Redeemer. May I see in the Baby Jesus all of God in the flesh.

I stand in humble reverence before Your almighty power that made it possible for You to be the Son of Man and the Son of God at the same time. Help me to treasure You as the greatest Christmas gift I receive, the Gift that will last forever, the Gift that gives me heaven. I thank You for giving Yourself for my sins and for bringing about true peace on earth between me and my heavenly Father.

Make me to grow in faith toward You and love toward my fellow men regardless of race. Grant me the true Christmas spirit of giving myself to You by giving my help to those in physical or spiritual need. Give me the boldness and courage to follow the example of the shepherds of Bethlehem, that I may tell my unchurched friends and loved ones of Your salvation, also for them.

May the bells of Christmas ring out throughout all the world. Help me to celebrate a spiritual Christmas in word, prayer, and song. Let the joy of Christmas abide in my heart all year long. All this I ask for Your sake, O dearest Jesus. Amen.

New Year's Day

O Lord Jesus, You are wonderful. I can never thank You enough for all Your blessings, and yet I come to You asking for more.

The new year is here again, and many things bother me. I would like to be popular with my friends. It is important to me that I get along well with others. So often I am misunderstood by my parents, teachers, and even my friends, and I so often misunderstand them. My schoolwork is often difficult for me. I really want to do well. I like to have fun, too. It seems that I cannot with a clear conscience do many things that others do.

If it is Your will, help me with all my troubles. Make me want to do what is right, and give me courage to say "No" when that is necessary. Help me to keep my good resolutions. Forgive my sins, keep me as Your child, and teach me to live this year, knowing that my time is in Your hands. Take my hand and lead me Your way, O Jesus. Amen.

Lent

O Savior of the world, in this Lenten season I think especially of Your great love for me and all humankind. Without You this world would be without hope. The terrible story of sin and guilt and death frightens me. But I know You have made everything right that was wrong. With You I find peace. Because of Your great sacrifice on the cross the devil lost his power over me. I am Yours, and as Your child I am safe.

Teach me to love You ever more, Lord Jesus, so that I will have a greater desire to serve You in the great work of Your church on earth. Give me courage to speak for You without fear. I am much too hesitant about telling friends about You and about asking those who do not know You to attend church services with me. I pray, give me the desire and ability to invite them to worship with me. Help me thus to tell others the good news of Your atoning sacrifice. In Your gracious name I ask it. Amen.

Easter

O living and victorious Savior, thank You for Your victory over sin and death. Send Your Holy Spirit to renew my faith in Your power. When I am weak and doubt Your love, appear to me through Your Word as You did to doubting Thomas. When I fall into temptation, because I forget to draw on Your help, appear to me as You did to Peter. When I am afraid because I do not use or trust Your Word, appear to me as You did to the frightened disciples in the locked room.

Give me faith to know that the Bible account of Your death and resurrection is true; faith that Your death freed me from sin; faith that because of Your resurrection I shall rise from the dead; faith that I shall live with You forever.

Grant that Your Easter victory may be my comfort and joy in life and in death. Hear my prayer, O living Lord and Savior. Amen.

Ascension Day

Lord Jesus Christ, on this Ascension Day I want to sing "Alleluia" with all my fellow Christians. Heaven is also my home, and that is where I want to be.

Keep me in the saving faith, and help me withstand all temptations and trials. Pray for me that my faith may never fail. Keep me reminded of Your bitter suffering and death, through which You have earned the joys of heaven for sinful mankind. Help all people to believe that they are redeemed and that You want them to share heaven with You.

You have promised: "Peace I leave with you, My peace I give unto you. . . . Let not your heart be troubled, neither let it be afraid." Lord Jesus, give me Your peace; remove all worries and cares from my heart; give me courage to face life as it is; and help me always look forward to being in heaven with You.

Prepare a place for me and for all believers as You have promised. And when death comes, give me joy in knowing that all my troubles will be turned into everlasting joy and that I will be with You. Hear me, dear Savior. Amen.

Pentecost

Lord God, Holy Spirit, pour out Your love on me and on all people this Pentecost Day. When I think of the three thousand whom You converted on the first great Pentecost, I marvel at Your power. I marvel still more when I think of the millions of people whom You have brought to faith and eternal life since that time, including me. Thanks for Your mercy.

Help me to watch and pray that I do not fall into temptation, or, when temptation comes, that I do not give in to sin. Draw me ever closer to my heavenly Father, to My loving Savior, and to You, the Giver of faith and the Sanctifier of my life. Make me a willing and able servant of God and my fellow men, especially my fellow Christians; help me to appreciate my parents, my brothers and sisters, and my friends; and make me kind to everyone.

Warm the hearts of the unbelievers, and give them faith in their wonderful Savior Jesus Christ, that they may share heaven with God and the holy angels and with all believers. Show me how I may by Word and example, and by the right use of my talents and possessions, help others find the way to heaven; through Jesus Christ. Amen.

Independence Day

Gracious God, Ruler of heaven and earth, for the protection and safety of our country You have given us the officials of our Government. They are Your servants, who are to rule according to Your will for the prevention and punishment of wickedness and for the maintenance of peace and order. Fill them with wisdom and understanding, loyalty and devotion, and help them to perform their task well. Give our officials a rich measure of faith and trust in You, and a love for Your saving Word, and use them to rule according to Your good pleasure.

Help me and all others to regard them always as Your representatives, to respect them, to obey them and the laws which they have made for the welfare of us all. If it be Your will, preserve the liberties which our nation has enjoyed since it was founded, and which have made it possible for us to prosper and for our church to flourish in peace. I ask it in the name of Jesus, the King of all kings. Amen.

Birthday

O Lord, give me grace to remember You, my Creator, on my birthday — that You have given me life for a purpose; that You have protected me from danger; that energy and interest in life come from You.

May I remember with faith in the days of my youth — my birthday by Baptism into life in Christ; the work of Your Spirit in my heart through the Word; the love of Jesus, who gave Himself for me.

May I remember with thanks in the days of my youth — loving hands of caring parents in my infancy; hands of dear ones folded in prayer for me; hands worn with toil to provide food, home, education.

May I remember with sorrow in the days of my youth — days spent without a thought of Your presence; moments of thoughtless rebellion and careless work; weeks wasted with willful selfishness.

May I remember with joy in the days of my youth — the forgiving love of my Savior; the promise of help for all my years; the call to live this year and every year in Your service.

May I remember You, O Lord, in the days of my youth. In the name of Jesus. Amen.

PRAYERS *on the Commandments*

For the Right Love for God

Dear Lord, I find it very hard to keep from making gods out of popularity, clothes, personal appearance, and exciting times. These are the things that seem so terribly important in my life, especially at school and at the corner drugstore. When I let myself make these things too important, I confess that I am really beginning to worship myself with all my heart, soul, and mind. Forgive this sin for Jesus' sake.

Help me to look at things differently. Help me to understand You better and to give You the place which You deserve in my life. Make my love for You stronger than my love for the things of this world. Help me to realize that You are the one really important thing in my life and that You will still be important after friends, clothes, good looks, and earthly pleasures are gone.

Give me the joyful assurance that You are mine and that I am Yours, that You are my Father and that I am Your child, and in that assurance help me to serve You day by day. In that assurance help me to look forward eagerly to the joys of heaven. Amen.

For Reverence

Lord God, I am thankful that I have become Your child by faith in Jesus Christ. I know that I owe my salvation to You alone. Your name means love and pardon to me. Grant that I may always treat Your name with the respect and reverence it deserves and to honor Your name as I try to honor You.

Some of the folks at school and in the neighborhood seem to think that people are grown-up and smart when they use the name of God to "spice up" the conversation with curses and oaths. Grant that I may not fall into the habit of using Your holy name in such profane and sinful ways. Where I have sinned in this respect, forgive me for Jesus' sake. Help me to remind my friends to use chaste and reverent language and to set them a good example.

Give me courage to stand up for what is right, even if it means that I will be ridiculed by those who do not know and love You as I do. Grant all this for Jesus' sake. Amen.

For Joy in Worship

Dear heavenly Father, I thank You for the inspiration that comes to me when I worship in church with my fellow Christians. I feel an inner peace when I hear You speaking the wonderful message of salvation in the Word which is read and preached. And it is a joy for me to express my thoughts to You in the hymns, in the prayers and in the liturgy. A church service is like a pleasant visit with You. Help me always to find it so.

Grant that my love for You and the Savior may grow stronger, so that my love for Your Word and my joy in worship may also increase. Give me the desire to attend church and Bible class on Sunday mornings, even when I am tempted to remain in bed to rest. In Jesus' name help me to find my rest in the comfort which You bring to the sin-burdened heart. Amen.

For Obedience to Parents

Dear Father in heaven, thank You for my parents, who guide and lead me in ways that are pleasing to You. Teach me to recognize Your guiding hand in all their dealings with me. Help me to accept their guidance with a respectful and thankful heart. Let me always remember that they are seeking my earthly and eternal welfare.

I want to show my parents the same honor and respect which Isaac showed to his father and which all Christian young people show to their parents. Grant me grace to give them honor, to serve and obey them as I should. Teach me to find joy and happiness in being kind and helpful to my parents. I know that is what You expect of me and what You will help me do. Help me to please my father and mother. Bless them for the many sacrifices which they have made for me.

Give our family a Christian spirit of love and understanding, and protect and guide us in all our ways. Keep us in the saving faith and finally take us all to heaven.

Grant these blessings in the name of Jesus, my Savior. Amen.

For Love for the Neighbor

Heavenly Father, out of love for me You have sent Jesus to be my Savior. I am thankful for that, and I want to show my love for You by loving my neighbor. Keep me from harming anyone by hand, mouth, heart, or mind. Help me to bear patiently the wrongs that others do to me. Grant me a forgiving heart that I may not try to gain revenge. Let no angry thoughts arise in my mind, and guard my tongue from angry words.

Fill my heart with love for my Savior that I may show love to others by being kind and helpful to them. Help me to be a good example to others, and use my good example to bring them to know Jesus. Guide all my thoughts, words, and actions that all my doings may bring honor and praise to Your name and good to my friends and neighbors. Take us all to heaven in Your own good time.

Grant these blessings for the sake of Jesus. Amen.

For Purity of Heart and Life

Dear God, with David I thank You for my wonderful body and mind. Thank You for the ability to work and play and to do good things for You and for my loved ones. I want to keep my body and mind pure and clean. To do so, I need Your help daily. Create in me a clean heart, and renew a right spirit within me. Fill me with holy thoughts, so that I will be right. Fill me with clean thoughts, so that I will be pleasing to You. Fill me with thoughts of love for You and others, so that I will be helpful and useful.

Wherever I have sinned with evil thoughts or evil deeds, forgive me for Jesus' sake. Wash me, make me clean. Make me white as the snow, and daily give me the comfort that all is well between You and me. When temptations arise, help me to overcome them by thinking of You and Your Word. I need Your help and the help of Christian people for this. So I pray, give me good Christian friends who are pure and wholesome. Help my friends and me to enjoy life together, and give us the joys which You approve.

Yes, Lord, help me to be what You want me to be. Help me to live the way You want me to live; through Jesus Christ. Amen.

For Honesty

Dear Father in heaven, Giver of everything good, accept my thanks for the many blessings which You have so lovingly and richly given to me. I confess that I deserve none of them, so please forgive me the many times I have shown my ungratefulness by grumbling or complaining. May the Holy Spirit strengthen my faith, that I may more fully appreciate Your many gifts and increase in thankfulness.

May I never take or keep anything which is not rightfully mine. Give me a sharp sense of distinction between what is mine and what is my neighbor's, and make me strictly honest in all things. Keep me from ruining my neighbor's property in any manner whatever. May I use my money and goods to Your glory and for my own and my neighbor's welfare. Give me a heart which is content with what I have and which rejoices when I see my neighbor prosper.

I ask this for the sake of Jesus, my Savior. Amen.

For a Kind Tongue

Dear God, how valuable is a good reputation! When Absalom spoke evil of David, he nearly brought his father to destruction. When Jonathan spoke well of David, he saved his life. Make me more and more like Jonathan. Give me a kind tongue. Help me to uphold the good reputation of others and to speak up for them, even when it is hard to do it.

Forgive me, Lord, for not always speaking up for people as I should. Forgive me for being so ready to judge them at times and for having a mouth that is so quick to speak evil. Forgive all lying and evil speaking of which I may have become guilty, and undo the harm I have done.

My mind and mouth are Yours, dear Lord, along with all the rest of me. Give me a kind heart and a loving tongue, and help me to think and say good things about everybody. Fill me with Your love, and let me make people happy by helping them in word and deed. Show me the good in people, and give me the courage to praise their good points. I pray in Jesus' name. Amen.

For Contentment

My good and generous God, I thank You because You have given me many good things, though I have not deserved a single one of them. This is especially true of my salvation which You have given me through faith in Jesus Christ.

Show me how fortunate I am to have all that I have — loving Christian parents, a happy home, a good education, plenty to eat and drink, good clothes to wear — and above everything — my church and Bible class which help to draw me closer to You.

Help me to be happy with what I have and not to waste even a minute wanting something I cannot or should not have, either because it belongs to someone else who wants to keep it or because it is out of my reach. Keep me from trying to get anything in a wrong way. When You give me more than I need, make me glad to help the less fortunate. Make me contented, knowing that I have everything I need on earth, and that also my eternal salvation is sure; through Jesus Christ. Amen.

PRAYERS *on the Petitions*
of the Lord's Prayer

That God's Name May Be Hallowed

Lord Jesus, Your name is holy, and I want to keep it holy by learning Your Word and by living a holy life according to it. When I am afraid, when I am lonely when I am discouraged, it is a sign that my faith in Your promises and my obedience are not what You desire. I do not then hallow Your name. O Lord Jesus, this should not be. For I cannot be happy or at peace without Your name — on my lips always, in my mind, and in my life

Let Your name be hallowed in me, Lord Jesus. Let Your name be more to me than my own name. Keep me from ever using Your name in a sinful way. Let Your name bring to my memory all that You have done for me — from eternity to Bethlehem, to Golgotha, to eternity. Let Your name bring to my mind all that You are: my beautiful Savior, Companion, and King.

To You I give myself, what little I am. To the hallowing of Your name I dedicate my life, O Jesus Christ, Messiah, Redeemer, Prince of Peace, King of kings and Lord of lords, and Lover of my soul. In Your name I pray Amen.

For the Coming of God's Kingdom

Lord Jesus Christ, You are my King. You are my only King. I follow You. I love You. I want to give myself completely to You.

That is why I pray for Your kingdom to come in all its grace and power and glory, because nothing else matters so much to me as seeing Your throne at the head of the world and Your Christians all together in front of You, and because longing for Your kingdom keeps me from fearing anyone or anything else.

Only You — my one King — only *You* I fear forever!

Lord, send Your kingdom soon! Meanwhile I will fear no evil, for You are with me . . . even to the end of the world.

I wait for You, my King. Even so come, Lord Jesus! Amen.

That God's Will May Be Done

Willingness to follow You, my Lord, does not come easy to me. I am no Abraham, quick to leave even his homeland to go where You directed. I am no Peter, quick to walk even those first steps across the water to grasp Your hand.

But, my Lord, I want to grow more and more willing to do whatever You will. So I pray You to make me more sensitive to Your will as I study Your Word and pray. When I have disappointments, help me to bear them. When I have sorrow, make me strong. When I am confused or lost, take my hand in Yours, bid the waves be still, and let me rest. Your will be done in me. Your will be done now and evermore, on earth as it is done in heaven. Take my life, fill it brimful with Your will, and hold me secure.

I take up my cross, Lord Jesus Christ, to follow You. Let Your will be my will. Amen.

For Daily Bread

Dear Father in heaven, through Jesus my Savior, You have given me eternal life. Each day You also give me what I need for my body. You are the gracious Giver of food, clothing, home, parents, property, employment, relatives, good friends, neighbors, good government, good weather, peace, a healthy body and mind, and honor. Thank You, dear Lord, for giving me all these blessings as I need them, even though I have not deserved them.

Lord, help me to understand that all blessings come from You, even though they seem to be a direct result of my work. Help me to remember that it is You who gives health, intelligence, and the opportunity to work and to earn a living. Make me patient in learning, so that I may prepare myself well for my life's work. Help me to serve others and thus to glorify You. Make me satisfied with what You have given, and help me to use Your gifts wisely for myself and others.

Grant all this for the sake of Jesus, my Savior. Amen.

For Forgiveness of Sins

Dear Father in heaven, You have given me so much that I can never thank You enough. Health, food, clothing, parents, friends, home, church, school, and all other blessings are from You. And yet I have given You so little in return. For this I am sorry and ashamed. Every morning I rise with the desire to love and obey You above all things, and every evening I have to confess my failures. It is humiliating to think that I deserve none of Your blessings. It is terrifying to think that I deserve only eternal damnation. But it is comforting to know that Your Son, Jesus, has taken the punishment of my sins. Father, forgive me for His sake, and make me sure of forgiveness and heaven. I know You will do it, because You love me.

Make me so happy about my own forgiveness, Lord, that I gladly forgive those who sin against me. Make it a real, heartfelt forgiveness. Enable me to pray for my enemies and to be loving and kind toward them. Show me opportunities to do good to other people. Make me able and willing to lead them to You, the forgiving God. Help me to do all this in thankfulness for Your mercy in forgiving me; through Jesus Christ. Amen.

For Help in Temptation

Lord God, heavenly Father, strengthen me to withstand all temptations which endanger my Christian faith. Let the truths of the Bible serve as a beacon to light my way safely through the many temptations which I must face every day. Help me boldly to answer those who tempt me: "How can I do this great wickedness and sin against God?" Help me also to remember Your promise: "I will not tempt you above that you are able."

Stretch forth Your mighty arm to deliver me when I sin, as I do every day. Teach me to realize that Your saving love will overcome even the worst of my sins. Forgive me for the suffering and sorrow which my sins have caused Your Son Jesus.

O Lord, I thank You also for the many occasions on which Your Holy Spirit gave me the strength to resist temptation and sin. Multiply these occasions, and help me to let my light so shine before men that I may become an example to others; through Jesus Christ. Amen.

For Deliverance from Evil

Dear heavenly Father, I come to thank You for the forgiveness which I have received through Your grace. I pray, always keep me in Your care and defend me against all danger. Keep me close to You by Your Word. Help me to use it, understand it, and love it. Keep me close to You through the Lord's Supper. By it assure me of Your love and care. Keep me close to You by prayer. Help me to pray earnestly and confidently for all my needs, and to praise You daily for Your goodness. Send Your Holy Spirit to protect me and to keep me safe.

And as I pray to be delivered from evil without, so I pray to be delivered from the evils of my own sinful heart. Give me victory over temptations. Keep me from becoming lax in my devotions and prayers, lest the old Adam within me lead me away from Your grace.

Help me to bear patiently such evils as will come. Grant that all trials and tribulations which You choose to send me will draw me nearer to You, to Jesus, and to the Holy Spirit. I pray in Jesus' name. Amen.

PRAYERS *for the* Week

Sunday

Dear Father in heaven, as I begin this new week, accept my thanks for every gift which You have given me for my body, mind, and soul, and, especially, for giving me the saving faith and heaven.

I know that I am not always thankful enough, and I have not always made the most of Your blessings. Sometimes I even misused them. But I am sorry for my sins and ask for full and free forgiveness for Jesus' sake.

Bless the holy Christian Church and all its members on this day of prayer and praise. Guide and strengthen those who preach and teach the Gospel. Bless all Christians in their worship. Give also me open ears and an open heart to receive Your Word with joy. Give me the power to live according to it.

Make me a good and faithful witness to the Gospel throughout the week. Guide me in all I think, do, or say. Help me always to remember and to do Your holy will; through Christ, my Lord. Amen.

Monday

Dear Lord of life, each day I live under Your guidance and protection. The time I spend on earth has no meaning unless You give me direction and crown my life with blessing.

Make my heart and life pure this week. Make my weaknesses and sins known to me and, forgiving them for Jesus' sake, grant me a willing spirit to overcome them and to correct my faults. Be with me whether I am at work or at play, and teach me to understand and meet life's problems with courageous faith.

Guide and guard my loved ones, and watch over my fellow men everywhere. Bless those who have not learned the Gospel's beauty and power, and bring them to life and salvation.

Teach me to use my opportunities to reach out to those in need and to lead them in the way of truth; for Jesus' sake. Amen.

Tuesday

Gracious Lord, having made me Your child through Christ, You have promised me every blessing.

I thank You for all the wonderful things You have given me, particularly for the Savior. I thank You for assuring me of the forgiveness of my sins, of peace and joy, and eternal salvation. I thank You for leading me safely through dangers and temptations and for enriching my days with good things. I thank You for loving parents, for faithful pastors and teachers, for my home in a land that is prosperous and free, and especially for making me a member of the holy Christian Church, where I enjoy life and service with those who share my faith and hope. Bless us all, Lord.

Teach me to show my gratitude always. Make my life happy and free from care by my trust in Your promises. Help me to be a witness to Your great goodness by my thankful conduct and speech; for Jesus' sake. Amen.

Wednesday

Dear Lord Jesus, my Savior, I have reached the midpoint of another busy week. As I look back, I must confess, dear Jesus, that I feel both sad and happy.

I am sad because even though I sincerely promised to be alert to temptations, I still permitted the devil, the world, and my sinful flesh to influence my thoughts, words, and deeds.

I am happy, however, because even though I have failed You, You protected me from evil. You gave me health, joy, good friends, and other blessings. Most important of all, You kept me in the true faith.

Forgiving Savior, You know my teen-age weaknesses, but You also know that I truly love You. Forgive my sins, make me strong in love for You, and help me to win victories for You every day.

Help me during the coming days to avoid following the lines of least resistance. Instead, strengthen me, and help me to worship You and to confess Your holy name. Make me helpful, useful, and kind, and in every way make me a living, walking, talking advertisement of the glorious Gospel. Amen.

Thursday

Almighty God, my heavenly Father, too often my life is self-centered. Today let me seriously consecrate my life to You.

Let me be an Enoch, who walked with his God. Let me be a Peter, who confessed: "Lord, You know that I love You." And when the many temptations of youth confront me, help me say with Joseph, "How can I do this great wickedness and sin against God?"

Holy Spirit, I especially ask You to give me a believing heart which will never question Your Word nor rebel against it. Instead, let me feed upon Your Word daily so that I may grow in grace and in knowledge of my Lord and Savior.

Use the vitality of my youth according to Your good will, and impress on me that to preach the Gospel I need also to live it.

Be with me, bless me, bless all people, let me be Yours forever. In Jesus' name. Amen.

Friday

Heavenly Father, I thank You for the gift of another day, and I pray that I may use it in a way that is pleasing to You. Help me to develop the wonderful mind and body that You have given me, so that I may be able to use my talents to do Your will and be of service to others. Give my teachers wisdom and patience, and give me an attentive mind and a willing heart. Let me see Your power in the laws of the universe and Your guiding hand in the affairs of men.

Through the death of Jesus on that other Friday I have been redeemed from sin and death. In love and thankfulness, may I live this day to You, my Creator, to Jesus, my Savior, and to the Holy Spirit, my Sanctifier.

> *Love so amazing, so divine,*
> *Demands my soul, my life, my all! Amen.*

Saturday

Heavenly Father, accept my thanks for the blessings of my Christian home. Show me how to be helpful and considerate to my parents, to understand their viewpoint and appreciate their concern for me.

Help me to use my leisure time in a way that is pleasing to You. In my work and play help me to remember that You are always with me to guide, to help, and to protect me.

Forgive my sins of the past week. Give me the assurance that You are always ready to forgive, and that all my sins have been washed away by the blood of Jesus.

And tomorrow, may the Holy Spirit open my heart to hear Your Word, that I may

See You more clearly,
Love You more dearly,
Follow more nearly
My Savior and Guide. Amen.

Luther's Morning Prayer

In the name of the Father and of the Son and of the Holy Ghost. Amen.

I thank Thee, my heavenly Father, through Jesus Christ, Thy dear Son, that Thou hast kept me this night from all harm and danger; and I pray Thee that Thou wouldst keep me this day also from sin and every evil, that all my doings and life may please Thee. For into Thy hands I commend myself, my body and soul, and all things. Let Thy holy angel be with me, that the wicked Foe may have no power over me. Amen.

Luther's Evening Prayer

In the name of the Father and of the Son and of the Holy Ghost. Amen.

I thank Thee, my heavenly Father, through Jesus Christ, Thy dear Son, that Thou hast graciously kept me this day; and I pray Thee that Thou wouldst forgive me all my sins where I have done wrong, and graciously keep me this night. For into Thy hands I commend myself, my body and soul, and all things. Let Thy holy angel be with me, that the wicked Foe may have no power over me. Amen.

Table PRAYERS

Before Meals

Heavenly Father, bless this food so that it will give me strength to serve You day by day.

May I never thoughtlessly waste any of the gracious gifts of Your divine mercy.

Help me to appreciate Your blessings more fully and to realize that all good things come from You.

In Jesus' name I ask this. Amen.

After Meals

Heavenly Father, help me to be truly thankful for the food which I have received through Thy goodness. Through this food and through the Bread of Life keep me in good health of body and soul. Nourish and strengthen body and spirit that I may be the better able to serve You; in the name of Jesus. Amen.

God, the Merciful Giver

The eyes of all wait upon Thee, O Lord, and Thou givest them their meat in due season. Thou openest Thine hand and satisfiest the desire of every living thing. Ps. 145:15, 16.

O give thanks unto the Lord, for He is good; for His mercy endureth forever; who giveth food to all flesh; for His mercy endureth forever. O give thanks unto the God of heaven; for His mercy endureth forever. Ps. 136: 1, 25, 26.

Miscellaneous PRAYERS

For Giving Myself Completely to God

I find it hard, dear Lord, to give myself to You completely. Each morning I promise faithfulness, honesty, kindness, and love. But too often the day is filled with proof that my prayers are only words.

I must submit to You, dear Lord. I know that You are the only Way to heaven. I realize there is no hope in anyone else. You are the Lamb of God that takes away the sin of the world.

Help me to submit completely to You, dear Lord. Give me the strength to give Myself to You. Teach me the sureness of Your love. Show me the wisdom of Your way of living.

I want to submit completely to You, dear Lord. Listening to Your Word, drawn by Your love, moved by Your Spirit, I will think and dream and work and play for You that I may truly be Your own and live under You in Your kingdom. And I look joyfully toward a life in heaven with You.

Now, with the help of the Holy Spirit I will submit to You, dear Lord. Amen.

For Joy in Being a Christian

Lord God, I am not always thankful enough that I am a Christian. When I stop to think of all the blessings that come to me because I believe in You, I can only say that Your love for me is the greatest thing that has ever happened to me. Make me properly thankful for Your love, and let me never fail to be happy about it.

Help me to find real joy in worshiping You in church. Help me to sing the truths of the wonderful hymns with my heart as well as with my lips. What I hear with my ear, send down deep into my heart. Let the joy of belonging to Jesus show itself in my words and actions, and make me a blessing to my family and friends.

Help me also to share my joy of salvation with others. So many people are discouraged and disappointed over both little and large matters. Help me to say and do the right thing at the right time, that my friends may also find their happiness in Jesus on earth and joy with Him in heaven. Bless me in this for Jesus' sake. Amen.

For the Conversion of the Unbelievers

Dear heavenly Father, I am grateful that You have from eternity desired to make me Your own and that You have granted me the forgiveness of sins, life, and salvation through my faith in Jesus Christ, Your Son.

All about on every hand, at home and everywhere in the world, multitudes of my fellow men of all colors, classes, and conditions in life do not yet know and accept Christ as their Redeemer from sin, death, the devil, and damnation. For all these persons — young and old, rich and poor, learned and illiterate, friend and foe alike, I pray. They are without God and without hope in the world. Call them out of the darkness of unbelief into Your marvelous light. Help them to believe in Jesus, who loved and gave Himself for everyone, and help them finally to obtain the glorious inheritance of heaven. I ask it in the name of Jesus. Amen.

For the Church

Blessed Lord Jesus, before Your ascension into heaven You said: "Go ye into all the world, and preach the Gospel to every creature." In this work of Your church on earth I want to help. Show me ways to take part in it, and make me glad to help in teaching Your Word. Make all Christians willing to participate in teaching the Gospel. Bring many people to faith and salvation, and save them from damnation. Help them to see that You are God and that with You they are blessed.

Give success to every Christian endeavor which is dedicated to the teaching of Your saving Word. Grant our missionaries, pastors, teachers, and all other workers of the church, power, perseverance, faithfulness, love, zeal, and success in their ministry of the Word to the sin-sick masses of humanity. Send forth many more laborers into Your abounding harvest of blood-bought souls. Build the spiritual strength of all Christian congregations, and enable Your people to grow in the grace of giving their time and money for the expansion of missionary activity everywhere. Help me to grow in this grace, too. In Your name. Amen.

For a Creative Life

Savior, You have set me into a time loud with the noise of destruction. I see people, and property, and possessions ruined by war, hate, greed, lust — violence of all kinds. I see how many lives are spent doing this destroying, and how few lives are lived to build, to bring healing to others, to create beauty and love, and make our land a happier place to be.

Lord, I want one of those creative lives for myself — a life packed with energy for doing good. When it is all done, I want to look back on it and see a building built with kindness, sympathy, understanding, and help. Only You can really build this building of my life. I know that. So really I am praying for more of You to crowd out of my heart every bit of blackness that would hurt my friends or You.

Build my life strong, dear Savior. Make it into a spiritual skyscraper — towering high, with Your name written bold on it. Amen.

Thanks for the Gift of Heaven

Lord Jesus, I am thankful that I have learned to believe You are my Savior and that I will go to heaven when I die. That means more to me than anything on earth.

Now, I pray, keep me always in the saving faith. Help me to love my parents and to respect them and all others who are over me. In fact, help me to do all that You want me to do as a Christian and as Your follower.

I ask You also to forgive me when I do wrong. Help me always to come to You when I have sinned. Do not let me forget about You, Jesus, and always make me sorry for my sins. Help me every day to try again to do what is right. With Your help I know I will be able to do it.

Keep me as Your very own, and help me to get to heaven by believing in You, dear Jesus. Keep me from attaching my heart in a sinful way to the things of this earth, and help me to look forward with real joy to an eternity with You and the holy angels and with all who die in the saving faith. Amen.

Thanks for Being a Christian

Dear God, I give thanks to You that I have found out about You and Jesus from my parents and from my pastors and teachers. I am glad I know that Jesus died for my sins and that I am saved. Keep me always happy, grateful, and humble about that, and help me to appreciate my Christian training more and more.

Of course, I do not at all times show that I am glad I am a Christian. For this I am sincerely sorry. Forgive me, Lord Jesus. I do not always talk or think like a Christian. For this forgive me, Lord Jesus. Yes, I often do not act like a Christian. For this, too, forgive me, Lord Jesus.

But I am glad I am a Christian, and I want to think and say and do the things which Christians should do. Therefore I pray, continue to be with me and help me at all times to love You, Lord Jesus, and to do Your will. Amen.

For the Blessings Through Baptism

Dear heavenly Father, I speak joyfully because I know You love me, because through Baptism You have made me a member of Your family. I thank You for all the rich blessings that are mine because I am baptized — for the forgiveness of my sins, for saving faith in my Savior, Jesus, and for the ability to live a God-pleasing life. Like the man of Ethiopia after his Baptism, I go on my way rejoicing. I have not earned these blessings, but You have given all as a free gift of Your great love for me. For this accept my sincere thanks.

I am sorry that I often sin against the promises I made at my Baptism. Forgive me these sins for Jesus' sake. Send Your Holy Spirit to strengthen me in my faith and in the power to fight all sins and temptations. Give me a joyful hope in Your promise of eternal life. Help me lead others to You that they also may receive the everlasting blessings of Baptism; in Jesus' name. Amen.

Before the Sacrament

Dear Lord Jesus, I ask Your blessing before receiving Holy Communion. I need Your guidance and help that I may take the Sacrament in a God-pleasing manner.

My heart is thankful and happy that I am a Christian and that I can receive Your love and forgiveness in the Holy Supper. I know I often sin in my thoughts and words, and in the things I do. I am sincerely sorry for all my sins, Lord Jesus. In faith I ask You to forgive me.

As I receive Your body and blood with the bread and wine, I pray for the gift of a stronger faith and for power to live a better Christian life. Your love gives me every blessing necessary for my body and soul. Help me to show my thanks in greater love and service to You, and in greater love and peaceableness toward the members of my family and toward my friends. Hear my prayer, dear Savior. Amen.

Before the Sacrament

Great Savior crucified for me, give me Yourself through this bread and wine. Pour out Your presence on me, and feed me with Your Word. Thrill me with Your love, and give me more love for You through Your love for me.

For every way in which I have failed You, my Savior, I ask forgiveness. For every moment of dissatisfaction, unbelief, doubt, despair, I beg Your understanding and forgetting. Now, when I come to Your Table, I await the cool refreshment of Your hand on my forehead — and the still peace of knowing that I have found You here.

In Your name, in Your presence, in faith in the cleansing power of the blood of the Lamb once slain for me, Savior, I come. Amen.

A "Thank You" for the Beautiful World

Almighty God, my Father in Christ, I want to thank You for the warm sun, the refreshing rain, and for the moon and stars at night. You have made this world wonderful. It shows me how great You are, and how small I am. Lord, make me strong to do as You would want me to do.

I want to thank You also for the beauties of nature — the mountains, the oceans, the rivers and lakes; the verdant fields, the flowers, and the forests; the beauty of all living things.

If You have made this world so fair
Where sin and death abound,
How beautiful, beyond compare,
Will Paradise be found!

Dear heavenly Father, let me feel Your greatness here, and prepare me for Your glory in heaven. I ask this for the sake of the atoning blood of Jesus, my Savior. Amen.

Before a Trip

Highways make for good times, Lord, when You travel along with me.

I do not fear anything but being without You — so go with me every mile of the way.

Spread Your arms around me to protect me on the way. And lead me through this trip into even more thrilling experiences with You.

I love to go with You, Savior — to keep moving and traveling from mile to mile, day to day, year to year. I believe in Your presence with me, and I know that all will be right so long as You are near.

Be with me always on the long road ahead, my Lord Jesus! Amen.

For My Friends

I love my friends, Lord Christ. I want You to help them find the same happiness in You that I have found.

So often words don't come to me when I try to speak about You to them. Lord, give me the strength and courage to talk about You naturally, because You are my best Friend — and it *is* natural to talk about friends you love.

There isn't anything better I can give my friends than You. Help me to give You freely to all. And so make me a wonderful friend for my friends to know.

Pack their lives with Your kind of gifts, my Lord. I pray for them because I love them — and because I love You.

Have much love for all of us, Savior and Friend! Amen.

Make Me an Instrument of Peace

(PRAYER OF FRANCIS OF ASSISI)

Lord, make me an instrument of Your peace, that, where there is hatred, I may bring love; that, where there is wrong, I may bring the spirit of forgiveness; that, where there is discord, I may bring harmony; that, where there is error, I may bring truth; that, where there is doubt, I may bring faith; that, where there is despair, I may bring hope; that, where there are shadows, I may bring Your light; that, where there is sadness, I may bring joy.

Lord, grant that I may seek rather to comfort than to be comforted; to understand than to be understood; to love than to be loved.

For it is by giving that one receives; it is by self-forgetting that one finds; it is by dying that one awakens to eternal life.

Lord, make me an instrument of Your peace; for Jesus' sake. Amen. ADAPTED

81

Lord, Teach Me How

Lord, teach me, as Your faithful follower, how
To have fun without folly,
To be cheerful without vanity,
To have self-respect without pride,
To be strict without fanaticism,
To be relaxed without laziness,
To be serious without gloom,
To be friendly and not fickle,
To be sunny and not silly,
    Lord, teach me how. Amen.

AUTHOR UNKNOWN